Groundwork

James O'Sullivan

Published in 2014 by
Alba Publishing
Uxbridge, UK

www.albapublishing.com

Copyright © James O'Sullivan

ISBN 978-1-910185-03-2

No part of this publication may be reproduced, stored in a retrieval system or transmitted in any form or by any means without the prior written permission of the author.

Printed and bound by Clondalkin Group, Dublin, Ireland

For my parents, John and Judith

Acknowledgements

I owe a lot of thanks to a lot of people, and while a few are mentioned here, it would be utterly impossible to list them all upon a single page.

First and foremost, Kim Richardson, who made this happen.

I would like to acknowledge all those editors who saw some value in my work. Thank you to everyone at *The SHOp*, *Southword*, *Revival Literary Journal*, *Bare Hands*, *Skylight 47*, *The Weekenders Magazine*, *The Linnet's Wings*, *The Poetry Bus*, *L'Allure des Mots*, *wordlegs*, *Doire Press*, *Outburst Magazine*, *Bray Arts Journal*, *The Southern Star*, the Cork *Holly Bough*, and *Motley Magazine*. Editors to whom I owe a particular debt of gratitude include Anne Fitzgerald, Elizabeth Reapy, John Dolan, Dominic Taylor, John and Hilary Wakeman, Thomas McCarthy, and Dennis and Rene Greig.

Thanks to Denis Kennedy, Michael Sexton, Tanis MacDonald, Doireann Ní Ghríofa, Allan Peterson, Leanne O'Sullivan, Ó Bhéal's Paul Casey, and Pat Cotter, Director of the Munster Literature Centre.

I greatly appreciate those festivals and venues that have hosted me over the years, including the Cork Spring Poetry Festival, the Irish Writers' Centre, An Róisín Dubh, and the Canadian Federation for the Humanities and Social Sciences.

Finally, I would like to thank my mentors, Graham Allen and Órla Murphy.

Remember When	1
Carriage	2
Cain and Abel	4
Heroes and Prodigal Sons	7
The White Arab	8
Clowns	9
Sleeping Dogs	10
Where Tricks Are Played	11
Fair	12
Chicken Sandwich Meals	13
Leaving	14
Ellen	15
Road	16
Envy	17
Salt and Chlorine	18
Olive Groves	19
Cream and Sugar	20
Boards	21
Professors	22
Séamas	23
Anxiety	24
Stars	25
While You Were Dancing	26
November	27
Mauve	28
Youth	29
There are Spiders	30
Before You Were Born	31
Moll's Gap	32
Tuesday Morning	33
Waiting	34
Molly	35
Beret	36
Moulted	37
Dynamic	38
Kindred	39

Caffè Tostato	40
Processing Doubt	41
Flies	42
Allies and Keepers	43
Old Music	44
Aurora Borealis	45
The Pickle Jar	46
Itch	47
Artists	48
Poet's Market	51
Nonchalance	52
Human, Nothing More	53
Children's Ward	54
The Godless Riots	55
Busking in the Tate	56
Megaphones	57
Concerned Citizens	58
Learning to Skate	59

A man learns to skate by staggering about making a fool of himself.

Indeed, he progresses in all things by resolutely making a fool of himself.

– George Bernard Shaw

Remember When

They used to stop at every watering hole.
Had you a headache, you had it four hours.
A theory that would not go untested,
when the Bunsen burner was handed back –
they were boiling the Starbucks on it.
Whatever that was. Something new – not quite right.
He was over in Saudi Arabia.
One of them countries anyway.
Ireland's wasted its finest sons – bums
need to be put on seats after all; balls
caught and the harvest put to proper use.

It's all a lot of bother that, the driver
was there for driving, what concern
was it of his when there's watering holes
to be reached? None. He'd driven in better
times, carrying more precious cargo.
Now he carries fat pigs, reminded
of how their snouts had pressed too deep,
dazzled by bright lights and dumb
like animals, or humans who'd forgotten
what it meant to be human.
Where once he oversaw the passage
of generals and devoted fathers,
now he herded pigs. Pining for better
days, thirty years ago, *d'ya remember?*

Carriage

Sucking without care,
feet propped on paper
bags from Pennys –
a last performance
to mark the theatre's
final night; invites
forced into the palms
of unwilling patrons.
Tired from the commute,
slogging the heavy tomes
of make-up artistry –
slapping your wrist
as you guessed it.

Talking of acres
offered in April –
big gates; plenty money;
cattle on it; no grief.
Prodigal sons
that never left home.
Masters of an art
never mastered –
Mayo needed it more,
eighty-nine was the year.
Raised not on songs,
but with heroes
everyone knew.

Swans' and Kings' heads –
by God we're living now.
Memories well-rehearsed.
Strained wrists
on Galtymore – hard men,
self-proclaimed,
telling epics to pages

that wouldn't be read.
Polite grunts
between the rattles
that kept tough mothers'
sons from being spoiled
by poetic words.

It was kind of him
to share such wisdom,
draw their thoughts
from Debenhams
and Roches Stores –
it was much better.
Wearing his plaster
like a purple heart,
introducing others,
warning of their life
stories, as he gave
his, like he'd given
it each time he could.

Cain and Abel

Noon fell, coming upon
that seedy store facing
Leeside's sunken palace –

Brazen natives in
oriental skin
glibly chattering –

A bone to those
who sought a loaf
for their dim minds
and sharp instincts –

Two sat, deep in
shadow beyond
yellow chirping;
flickering forks –

Suspicion eyed all
who entered knowing
that the good should leave –

Little difference lay
between them, looking out
beyond their wiry cage –

Ears lay balanced, seeing
none whiter, only white
set in pink, just as red –

Greed forged many pools
by raw paws ready
to rip what they could –

Fat would be chewed
in blood; bargains
to wipe one's chin –
we all have chins –

Struggling to stand,
trying hard to pick
bone from bone, where
only bones lay –

Dead trees make for war
it seems, when branches
are split among men –

Tongues twist as brothers fell,
eyeing throats once followed,
made silent on that bend –

Swallows dance there now, paired
beneath willows with sleeves;
tangled roots; shallow soil –

Reflections of dear
friends that never were,
poisoned by promise –

Words from great men
divinely tasked with
delivering
God's brave children –

Mothers serving
tea twice daily,
passing lengths of
their own table –

Wasted sacrifice
consumed by goddess smiles
and charming peddlers –

Idle chairs cause grief;
fathers' fears; daughters' tears –
no brothers to be seen.

Heroes and Prodigal Sons

We almost made it.
West Cork's hero –
he almost made it,
his valiant effort
written off against
young intentions.

Fermanagh's lost boy,
given titles,
fair and fancy,
in Belfast –
titles to hang
on the walls
of spoiled mothers,
sons and daughters.

The prodigal son
returned to recoup
losses from mothers,
sons and daughters –
not his own.

The White Arab

Have you seen the white Arab,
flogging books down the river bank,
where Hadrian rots and statues
do what they should?
Ask a Cork man about statues,
they'll know the white Arab.
Sure enough. Buy a book,
he needs the pennies it seems,
but don't read – it's not for reading.

It seems.

Ask a Roman or a Venetian,
or a Corkman. They'll know.
They'll all know the white Arab,
by the river, flogging penny dreadfuls –
shielded from the grey sun.

Clowns

When you pay entry to the circus,
you hope to see the ringmaster,
but he was up in Mayo most days.

His guests, toffee stained,
wondered why he'd shy away,
watching clowns bicker on the left
and right of the oval stage.

That's the same elephant. It's not.
Get your peanuts! It's the same. No.
Peanuts for all! Peanuts, peanuts!

Sleeping Dogs

In Beaumont; on Maher Street
they wait, teased by white decay,
its steady, lingering spread.
Anschluss cannot be repealed
on plains that are not man-made.
Each morsel annexed, dark mass
driving toddlers down alleys.
In every city and bed they wait,
sucking on lemons.

There are others walking in temples,
free from dogma, spitting on those
whose chime forces them to rise
from their blue mist –
their place of enlightenment.

Where Tricks Are Played

In my unreliable eye he slept sounder,
on a bed of wool, with no perturb
for those who gladly chased thunder.
Once the root of that most vital heave,
gazed within tarnished frames, second hand –
winds may still – their burns remain.

He was sleeping then – he is sleeping now.

Empty, he lay on that ghostly glass,
flat, flowing, forever down, cast
by some strange soul we'd never know.
Then he was gone. Months later, another?
Surely I can recall there being two –
the one that wasn't and the one we knew.

It is here, and there, where tricks are played.

Fair

Crustaceans lined pots,
dry greasy pans
piled in the crevasse.
They could have dangled
in the light, directing
stragglers passing their way.

Older backs had been strained –
so to us they'd do the same.

Chicken Sandwich Meals

We ate chicken sandwich meals,
spoke of dreams like they were fears,
not our own, but passed along.

Counting the glyphs and pillars,
wrapped in cheap exotic scenes,
pooling barter for buttons,
more plentiful than our own,
from stained stripped shirts and blouses
damp with greasy heat that poured
into the skin of fools who spoke,
hushed, of dreams, passed along.

Leaving

Strange, that others recite
what the masters cannot.

Filthy, they stagger
in their own filth –
continuity for humanity,
the greater race.

Cockroaches, they gather
in dark corners, mating
to the taste and smell
of blood and cheap spirits.

Ellen

Her moment is set in a misty black and white,
or is it a sort of sepia? I don't even remember that.
She gave up colour for those that came after.

Her piano has been out of tune for decades,
but its timber still has a shine to it. A few keys stick.
She was a great composer. But never credited.

Road

Once, when she sat there,
it was grass and not a road.

Silence was not so easy
to mistake then. She waits.
It might come again, that time
when she was idle out of purpose.

Jerry, Thomas and the Stones
all lied to us. They know that now.

Envy

My mother made tea;
he went to turn his keys

and I buttered bread
for a Tayto sandwich.

Neither hung their heads.
Others took turns

on concrete floors
looking for something –

others had everything;
others had nothing.

Salt and Chlorine

Embracing, laughing, in salt and chlorine,
they spoke in Sardinian tongues,
with accents from the republic of bears.

Trading at whim, their bond was plain, tendrils
accompanied by coconut, constructed by men
who know how a scene should be seen.

Later, others lay awake,
with burned skin
that went unnoticed.

Olive Groves

Unspoiled dust – soil – red
perfection, painted –
no blemish on this dirt
making stomachs turn
against their nature.
There are no mergers –
no followers here –
a concern for silence,
smothering like breasts,
sweating without salt.

Cream and Sugar

We chose how we took our tea –
milk, sugar – no tea at all.
There was cream in coffee
Tuesday – Wednesday – black.
Cream and sugar –
black with sugar –
no sugar, no cream –
no coffee, no tea.

We never chose how
we broke our bread;
few drank white wine.

Boards

Shoes like chairs underfoot,
heated by the flu under drafty
windows, bog men on the mind.
Tight passageways emptied space
where guilty jesters pondered
tighter ways where they might
spread widely their guilty thoughts.
They spoke of Borris and places
of barter where tigers had never
been; chickens ran amuck for
children to feed and babies to eat.
Chickens were all those children
thought of – itchy limbs drove
thoughts to memories of men,
deep in the soil, and their meaning.
They thought of little else –
      not tigers, heat, nor cold.

Professors

They held us like they held themselves once –
the second chance of those who taught each
        word and step.

What was meant for the mind found itself
much deeper, where young women prompted
        old thinking.

We move forward, but with caution,
borne of steps we have already taken.

Séamas

I'd never any *scéil* for that fella,
that insisted he knew better
than my mother, who called me James.

Anxiety

That drum you couldn't hear
greet that hobbling smile –
gulls perched in urban shade
as fishermen whistled somewhere.

Pillows would have been sniffed
gladly; toes curled, eyes shut.

That grinding taste – chalky
now – glancing for safety
among scattered pages
passed by predecessors out there.

Stories of pressed trousers
to ease the restless pup.

Stars

Danny boy got his doctorate
the other day. *A lovely title.*

That other one got in *The Guardian* –
I'd not even know where to buy it.

Mothers have a thing for second place.
She went about her business as she did.

The stars could be all around you,
and still, you would reach for them.

While You Were Dancing

A black dress, holding
Eve's difference
with strange beats,
guiding alien hands
to food for starving
mouths – lips – that
would never taste it,
leaving bellies sick
while dragons lay idle
on vast tracts
of nowhere, among
mammoth spaceships
and silent temples.

November

That morning holds sway
over better days –
the air was colder.

Words for the wordless,
failing then and now,
toeing sticks and stones
on the frosty ground.

Acrylic pills, oversized
heirlooms – familiar
cracks, breaking dawn.

Whores sat on barrels,
dried grease – trenches
where children played
with saturated steel.

Those wounds remain,
though the earth
has been filled.

Mauve

Accountants in pink jumpers
lined with cheap table cloth,
defended by starving barristers –
a shortage of dainty loins –
offered closing statements,
pre-approved.

Flocking boobies tasked
with defunct crafts
pumped shades;
practised mating calls
rushed by misplaced
comfort, crossing
bridges without nails.

Youth

It was so simple, that twig from another world.
Hurled through infinity, resting now
in unfamiliar heat by a two-foot ocean.

Plastic companions buckled, gazing idly
down that splintered highway
that would have lasting or passing function.

Things then are here now, hidden in plain sight.

There are Spiders

He wore a long white coat
not to get chalk on his jumper,
and carried a plastic compass
so he could draw circles, but mostly
make a booming sound when we drifted.

We were a terrible bunch,
asking questions in ignorance,
beneath the lofty standards
of a man who had achieved much
and asked so little.

He had me once for drawing
with a pen – drawing is for pencils.
And I didn't rule my copy in advance.
The night before I hadn't slept,
for the fear of fearing spiders.

Before You Were Born

I saw your white face
on Hanover Street,
staring idly at idle feet.

You had no name.

Moll's Gap

She looked like she was down from the moors,
as opposed to out of the box, where she usually sat.

She made good use of that space, but it was just as well
that she took some clean air every now and again.

She showed me bog moss and taught me how it sucked
up all the Irish oak. I'll always know that path blind.

Tuesday Morning

Sticking, his finger traced
across tattooed timber –
sweat and beautiful filth.
Five sat in that corner,
ears ringing from music
turned to sound. Five, and her.
Speaking with sore temples,
bellowed whispers, inches
from that valley – lesser
men wiping the moisture
from their face, wandering
marshlands where few noble
creatures flirt with Avril.
Time wound itself gladly
in the mist, sour mash
and boiled blood in the pannes.
Nothing lay between them
but heaving space and all
that would hope to fill it,
in wait of lesser space
taken by much the same.

Waiting

Empty echoes take their chance –
nothings sift through gentle fingers.

Threading deep in warm sand –
There are larger seagulls here –
casting through the heat to bright
triangles in the summer fog.

Eating berries in the frost –
Snow has settled here before –
fingers do what they should not,
by brighter swords and chilled orchestras.

Her name must be soft.
Softer than the one I call.
Empty echoes take their chance –
nothings sift through gentle fingers.

Molly

She thanked me where Salmon lay watchful eyes,
undivided by those who sought iron gall ink,
with coffee cups to keep them on their way.

She wears too much of that stuff – the wall,
beneath the cracks, firm as one three years
in the building – knocked and restarted twice.
The scales on Salmon peeled easier. His flesh
wasn't quite as pink – it held no tannin.

She thanked me by those eyes forever fixed,
while I fixed on her a lasting stare that would
keep my own self pink when my mouth ran dry.

Beret

If you go by the hollow
where the Farnhams sat,
cast an eye for a quiet soul,
stood where birds hop,
in a wool beret, cast,
in sixteen shades of grey.
Do not let the cold
lead you astray,
her collar is high
but she welcomes embrace.
As you pass through the hollow,
so too will that face.

Walking with cattle
you'll be lost in a snare
if your find yourself
locked in that quizzical glare.
You'll see it again,
sat on dark hair,
the same as in any dream –
a beret, made of wool.
She'll offer you whiskey
to warm your throat,
and tease you with heaves
she doesn't even know.

You will wonder, if that hat
fits you better, than the one
you call your own.

Moulted

A half chime, a scene set.
Predators cosy in their mantle.
A smooth surface, no undergrowth;
cold serpents slithering
towards idle mechanical beasts.

It was Autumn. That matters little
where friction plies its trade.

Standing by beasts –
the serpent –
without need to shed
her iron oxide skin.
Beasts without gears
also lay in that cave –
the serpent would be
moulted. All the same.

Dynamic

Moss, strange to Boulogne-Billancourt,
speckled the gleam and grime.

Wires hung loose, rocking
to noises even stranger.

She counted each step, sweating,
on both sides, granting wishes –
as she could. No man turned to her.

Kindred

She heard her own body crack
with the glass that splintered
in the bloodied rain that took
the place of tears that might
once have been, but never came.
His thoughts were all that reached
his infant son before the future
walked indifferently away from
their mangled bodies, lying, still, apart.
She came this way several minutes
late and at the last request of her
boyfriend's disorganised charm.
He had come to do what he had
set out to do some other time,
but had instead been here,
not there, as we are, anywhere.

Caffè Tostato

Where man-made streams turn
and guitars are often plucked –
rarely sold – he walked,
sat, the past in view.
Exotic lands teased his toes,
buried in dark soil –
>*era ricco e caldo.*
Heinous heat from foreign suns,
built in foreign lands,
burned and cooled his face.
In that reckless carnival,
chatter formed its crest –
he saw the colour,
in rows, upon the wall –
red and orange – and red.
He'd not tempt himself
beyond that of his presence –
>*non avevano latte.*

Processing Doubt

The birds came out at two,
one winter, and in spring,
and again that summer.
Was it warmer then
when we tossed, congested,
stretching necks during
fantasies interrupted
by mucus coughs?
Brilliance at arm's length,
we listened to their song
in the misplaced hope
of bringing them closer.

Flies

Too many flies
entered that room
in the summer
when her darkness
was hard to see –
You knew the time
by the throbbing,
but knowing
and doing
are much like
flies and sleep
in the summer –
like your mentors,
driving you mad,
filling your bags,
bleeding you of
that foul odour.

Then you hunt them –
like flies.

Allies and Keepers

I knew a cartoon from a great city carved of ice,
or so it seemed, peering beyond the mono snow,
towering boldly, hand sculpted, greater
than any man or beast or otherwise.
Its cold walls seemed of bastard glass,
grey, content in having surpassed its makers –
it would not remember them despite their efforts.

I knew a cartoon once, who had been my host
as I lay beneath those towering ceilings,
almost on a horizon lost, unfit for their purpose
it would seem. I could not fly to that line,
as my host served me milk and meat and mead.
We would share tales of exploits, growing fatter
from our fill of false accomplishment.

I knew a girl from Babylon. Purple lips
under hair that consumed, a sharp jaw,
set against sharper hills and monotonous sand.
We'd sit in strange spaces, familiar places
sharing tales of other worlds in our world,
missing what we never had.
She had two names, caring only for one.

Old Music

You'd quiz the postman
'til you saw him;
then you knew
that kind of knowing.
They'd gone to work
on that block
in a jagged way.

Hauling eager bones
to a steely chariot,
weighed down by facts
that'd never be known,
listening to the
the only genius
to have found Jesus.

Aurora Borealis

Flowing to the summit
where Boreas blew warmth
and Aurora brought cold.

No mystics shed beauty,
or called from their swindle.

There is never just one.

The Pickle Jar

With poor timing we often pour coal upon the embers.
From the fridge I took the pickle jar. It barely fit in my palm.
It was heavy with that flavour so familiar to careless sons.
Memory seduces your tongue with ease, a siren in the dark,
made darker by the light of fridges, it would seem.

It builds, like any scene, to that moment, the villain revealed,
the maiden laid bare, spoils of war cast out to share among
soldiers whose brothers they bludgeon at every moment.
Always brothers. The anvil lifted – a sharpness in my palm –
I had a pickle jar to open. But the pickle jar would not.

Itch

She asked me if her mommy was going to be okay.
She had *itchy eyes*, and a terrible itch it was.

I let her have as much lemonade as she wanted,
piled on the ketchup, let her eat her chocolate first.

Will mommy be okay? I put on her favourite cartoon,
let her play with that expensive toy, rarely unboxed.

Artists

I

Composed in corduroy,
its origins were sound,
kept safe by false years,
draped on tired shoulders.

Sweating necks turned
to do this serious business,
recording condemnation
on cheap moleskins.

Every leaf has a place
on pruned trees,
sweeping towards thick
linear constructs.

Sharing eager words
that don't fit but demand
to be present, noting
every clear presence.

Shrugging off fools,
they are nameless
to those ignorant proles
yet to be enlightened.

II

Mary Magdalene's brush would have been fine,
and her work posted on Parisian walls.
There was never a shortage of tapestry in Babylon.
Praise the artist, forced to live off the spoils
of fat and greedy suits – too good for two cents,
robbed from fools whose idle minds

were beset by wilier fools, telling tales
of vampires and witches and childish things.

III

Kolyn looked like he'd none to spend –
he spent a lot of time at that.
It was Farran Ó Mhurchú – a k and a y –
Ó Mhurchú – sure that was his name –

He never leant on four walls –
if you didn't get it, it wasn't yours to get.
You could join them, or stay leaning –
smite the editor, but watch your tongue.

IV

She told me stories about her mother,
and some thing she'd used to wash out shirts;
hanging them by some orange cord
that stood in the garden – Arcadia itself.

That other one was angry – he'd been cut
by some simpler creature who didn't understand
that one day the world would know her folly.
These are the things that matter.

V

Fruit bowls are such trivial things
to be concerned with. What's a horse
if it doesn't have the voice of a man?

Why put a line down straight,
when you can wobble?
Lines were meant for free hands.

I'll take a walk to the tower someday,
but I doubt that I will get there,
and I'll be walking on my own –
      as others run.

Poet's Market

I remember that night on a Google Hangout,
talking with Joyce and Woolf and Pound –
Eliot was there too, I think.

The six of us listened so very contently,
as they told us about their process,
how it was *more physical than method.*

Woolf wanted something that jumped
in a lake – went wild – wasn't *safe.*
Joyce just wanted Joyce.

I can't remember what Pound said.
Eliot was there too, I think.

Nonchalance

Young men playing soldier
with tomes underarm
and collars finely pressed.

Sacred words from basalt pens,
slanting on luxury, telling
fables from beyond the Pale.

Rust won't shift her, slapping
down against the rot,
thighs heavy with the cold.

Engines ticking beyond, bent
by the bedside of boxers –
strewn on bloody cotton rags –
where it truly means something
to be afraid of the dark.

Sucking on straw, cursing
their lot on warm days,
cheated of their cents by
witless old-timers
tasked with providing their
due entitlement.

Idle words
out of the black –
words that speak –
addressed to all.

Human, Nothing More

No word should exist; they are not cattle
to be branded by more civilised keepers
whose cities are base, their world addled.
      They are human, nothing more.

Ostracised by the selective minds of preachers
whose divinity rings throughout stolen chapels,
enjoying the full pardon of timorous leaders,

they wait for hands not so idle, and facile
voices raised by more articulate speakers.
They have waited, but words are babble.
      They are human, nothing more.

Children's Ward

Would it make any difference if I wrote your name
like Ozymandias, or would you rather sit awake
waiting for toy soldiers, worried they might not come?
Should I tell of you by mossy stones, where you yourself
might want to climb, scrape your knee, and pine
for eyes, the colour of which you can't quite recall?
What if I put down your tale, for all to know –
would you rather touch Murano glass, taste chocolate
until you're sick, and stay up late watching cheap telly?

The Godless Riots

Contractual tea, poured
with words of certainty –
God had been cast aside,

had God been in their hearts
they would not have burned homes,
birth rights and livelihoods.

She allowed herself a nod,
with lips on fine china.

Busking in the Tate

Kicking hacky sacks as swans sought shelter
from the orange glow; gathering
their precious Belgian metals, thinking
they'd struck gold from the Zuiderzee.
Leonidas, each and every one,
staring down docile bards
who'd tell authentic tales first hand.
Busking in the Tate, sharing their banter
with bears, marking territory
sown by fools who sought to mark their own.

Megaphones

When they ran the lights all they did was laugh –
it was only daddy's car; some other daddy's boy –

"Her legs would smell good in the air."
"Is your dolly on the take?"

They took up megaphones, so they could scream,
and we would know that they had been failed.

Concerned Citizens

A few thousand of them came out in Ballyconnell,
the Anglo-Irish war was never short of martyrs.

They'd rise again, from the ashes, very phoenix like,
to hunt down those who had carelessly set the tinder.

There are always casualties of war, and six-bed houses,
and wedding cakes the price of the household average.

Learning to Skate

For Graham Allen

You told me a story once, of a Cork boy
with matted hair. He was running,
down a hill I knew, *away from the barracks*,
you said, kicking a can or a football or something.
Look at your auditorium, full of Cork's children.

You told me once that some men grow up
in public. Do you think it home now, here,
where we can see tractors laid to rest?
Or do you pine for Liverpool Street and Trasimeno?
Do you remember finding your way to Ferragosto?

It's interesting that you say *The Time Machine* –
where would you go? What would you say?
Would you bring Bloom his passage?
Would you fear he'd leave it to gather dust
upon a stack of monographs bearing his name?

James O'Sullivan's poetry has appeared in numerous periodicals and anthologies, including *The SHOp*, *Southword*, *Revival*, and *wordlegs*. His first collection of poetry, *Kneeling on the Redwood Floor*, was published by Lapwing in 2011. James, the Founding Editor of New Binary Press, is a graduate of University College Cork, University College Dublin, and Cork Institute of Technology. He has been a guest reader at such events as the Cork Spring Poetry Festival, and Canadian Federation for the Humanities and Social Sciences, and has received a variety of awards for his work. He is also a published journalist, photographer and digital artist, while his short fiction has appeared in, amongst others, *The Burning Bush 2* and the *wordlegs 30 under 30* anthology, published by Doire Press in 2012. As a publisher, he has produced collections by some of Ireland's most promising talents, such as Graham Allen and John Saunders, while his press has also hosted many accomplished authors as readers, including Eiléan Ní Chuilleanáin, Billy Ramsell, Gerry Murphy, and Leanne O'Sullivan.

Further information on James and his work can be found online at josullivan.org.